THE UNTOLD ONLINE LOVE STORIES

THE UNTOLD ONLINE LOVE STORIES

MARLON C. JONES

XULON PRESS

Xulon Press
2301 Lucien Way #415
Maitland, FL 32751
407.339.4217
www.xulonpress.com

Printed in the United States of America.

Paperback ISBN-13: 978-1-66280-449-6
eBook ISBN-13: 978-1-6628-0450-2

Table of Contents

Introduction

On these pages you will meet people. You will hear stories of despair followed by triumph, as well as stories of isolation leading to victory.

We are a family, an online family of believers, that live miles apart. We live in different time zones and on different continents. We are single, married, divorced, labeled by governments as disabled; we are people with children and without children; we are musicians, interpreters, and writers. We have diverse backgrounds and cultures, as well as various teaching experiences.

However, the one thing we have in common, and the reason I am writing this book is because we have all been given hope through a unique place. This hope we found together came through an online church experience. Because of this online experience, our lives have never been the same.

We have similar struggles and yet not so similar circumstances. But through it all, we have been there for each other through devices such as computers, laptops, iPads, and cellular phones. We communicate via Zoom Cloud Meetings, GroupMe app or WhatsApp. We even video chat with each other through Facebook messenger. Everything we do is through the "*virtual world,*" and it has been one of the most fulfilling experiences we have ever had.

I never would have believed just four years ago how significantly different my life would be or that I would meet the people that would help me through this life and spiritual journey. I would never have imagined that I would be talking to people like Dawn in Texas or Viv in London on a weekly basis. I would have laughed at the thought of meeting on Zoom to chat with individuals in Uganda, Poland, Sweden and Ohio. No one could have convinced me that I would be sending messages to a group of intercessors in an app asking for prayer for my family or for various activities throughout the hectic week.

It has made all the difference in my own journey and walk with God. He has opened my eyes to my own strengths and gifts, as well as His purpose. He has given me opportunities to step out and stretch myself. God has given me the courage to speak into people's lives through words that I never knew possible. He (God) has offered each one of us hope through stories and worship. I might never have been aware of His biblical truths had it not been for this amazing revelation. I am so thankful for the opportunity to unite with other believers, which I now lovingly refer to as family.

Community is so valuable. As we walk alongside one another in every moment, there are missteps to fall along the way, as well as an opportunity to build others up. As a group, we can depend on each other to reach out when we feel unstable. When we have strength, we can lend it to someone in need. That is exactly what our extended family exercises.

Our connection is not at a local church, homeless shelter, or volunteer organization. We meet each other on a screen, located somewhere in our own homes, vehicles, or coffee shops. We share joyous occasions or heartache; we pray and speak truth into the life of someone as much as three thousand miles away. This is what is so amazing about our connections. God is very intentional. What may be a tool of the enemy, He can and will turn for His good and His glory! What some may perceive as a tool meant to isolate and divide is truly a resource for bringing people together. (Romans 8:28) The internet has changed lives. Many lives, especially in Melanie's story about her and her son's journey.

I hope you enjoy reading about our journeys. My hope is that at least one of these stories (if not more) resonate with your individual situation as you face some of your own battles.

My desire is that you will find the hope we found as you continue to seek Jesus and follow

Him down your own individual paths. We have all found that His grace is enough for us. His strength is made perfect in our weakness. We have seen that His promises are true, and He will surround us. He is present in a meeting with two individuals or when we are alone in our bedrooms. He promises to never leave us nor forsake (Hebrews 13:5). He remains unchanging, unwavering, and will chase after the one who is lost because His mercies are new every morning. We have found that even when the world wants to tell us there is no way, He makes a way. When society tries to convince us of the things we think we need, He tells us *He is all* we need. And we have understood this to be true. We do not need a brick and mortar church with a steeple atop it to serve an almighty God. We do not need a set of chairs or an altar to worship our King.

The only thing He requires is a willingness that is pure and humble, a contrite spirit, and a desire to know Him more. He has given us the opportunity to do this. He has given you the opportunity as well... I hope you choose to follow the

steps He has laid out for you, much like we have. It has been nothing short of miraculous.

> **Now you [collectively] are Christ's body and [individually] you are members of it, each part severally and distinct [each with his own place and function]. —(1 Corinthians 12:27)**

CHAPTER I

OVERCOMER (MARLON)

> **You see, every child of God *overcomes* the world, for our faith is the victorious power that triumphs over the world.—(1 John 5:4)**

I WAS ON MY LUNCH BREAK ON FEBRUARY 10, 2012, talking to my older brother. It was his forty-fourth birthday and I thought lunch time would be a great time to call him. In hindsight, it was *perfect timing* for the birthday wishes. I was completely unaware that I would be spending my evening in the emergency room of a hospital located in Atlanta, Georgia.

Something was quite off with my body; in fact, things in my body had been off for a couple of months now. But in true male fashion, I continually put off looking into it as far as being "*medically concerned.*" On that chilly winter day, I thought to myself, "I'm going to the emergency room immediately after work!" I worked from 11AM-7PM EST at the time, so I arrived at Piedmont Hospital at approximately 8PM.

Hush-Hush

After waiting around for forty-five minutes, my name was finally called and off to the exam room I went. I told the attending person I had extremely low energy and had been feeling sluggish lately. After examining me, she said something to the effect of "*Given your very low blood count, I'm surprised you were able to walk back here.*" The hospital quickly admitted me, but at that point I was uncertain as to why. They suspected something serious, because I spent the first night in the ICU (Intensive

Care Unit), where I received two units of blood. Still no reason was given for my admission.

The next day (Saturday), I was moved to a regular hospital room where I was instructed to prepare for the colonoscopy scheduled for the upcoming Monday, February 13th. YIKES! I do not think I should describe that process to you, because I sense that many of you can already relate. That said, I will segue to another topic.

Later that day (February 11th, 2012), an icon and megastar suddenly passed away unexpectedly in Los Angeles. She also happened to be one of my very first celebrity crushes, so I was *devastated.* I even received two separate phone calls of consolation, as if a close relative of mine had suddenly died. Both my sister and a good friend of mine checked on me that evening, and then I announced to my friend that I had a massive headache and headed to bed. It was pretty early for a then thirty-seven-year-old to retire for the evening.

Diagnosis Day

On February 14th, after a series of tests (colonoscopy included), the doctor entered my hospital room with a straight face. She sat down next to me and said flatly, "Mr. Jones, all of your test results are back, and you have cancer." Given the discouraging news, one might surmise that I would have some sort of breakdown, but that is not what happened at all. In fact, a compliment came out of my mouth. I complimented the doctor on her shade of lipstick (orange).

In hindsight, I now believe she assumed I was in shock due to my response. She insisted I focus, as she repeated the words, **"You have cancer."** I calmly uttered, "Okay so what are the next steps?" I also thought to myself, "I am focused; just not on the disheartening news you just delivered to me."

The Journey Begins

I was administered two different chemotherapy treatments, as well as several lumbar punctures as a part of the regimen. The diagnosis was a rare form of cancer called Burkitt's Lymphoma. Abbey Lee Miller (the coach of the television show "*Dance Moms*" on the Lifetime network) was also diagnosed with the same type of cancer. My prognosis was not good... I would later find out I was in the final stages of the illness, being Stage IV.

The cancer was in my spine as well as my stomach, so the chemotherapy treatment was both intense and rigorous. I recall my oncologist writing seven procedures on a dry erase board that I would need to go through to complete the journey to remission. After going over the items, I shouted out very colorful language over the idea of completing the list of items. She shouted back an emphatic "NO," and remarked that together, we would beat this cancer diagnosis.

> **So be strong and courageous! Do *not* be afraid and do *not* panic before them. For the Lord your God will PERSONALLY go ahead of you.**

He will *never* fail you nor *abandon* you.—(Deuteronomy 31:6)

God kept His promise through my oncologist as well as several of the nurses and hospital staff. You see, I had truly little will to fight the cancer battle, let alone to exercise my measure of faith. But the Holy Spirit made it necessary for others surrounding me to believe on my behalf.

The fact that I was surrounded by love and warmth spoke volumes to me, because my blood relatives were in excess of eight hundred miles away. That love and encouragement, coupled with the relentless visits from one of my closest friends (Kevin W), undoubtedly led to the remission that I find freedom in today.

Little did I know that God was preparing me to find comfort in being surrounded by unlikely individuals with a unique set of circumstances. God was setting the stage for my new normal, and my *much*-welcomed ***online*** family.

Don't be afraid for I am with you. Don't be discouraged, for I am your God. I will strengthen you and help you. I will hold you up with my victorious right hand.—(Isaiah 41:10)

O Ye of little faith

During the next seven months, I became awfully familiar with the hospital staff. I frequently endured hospital stays. Most were planned for chemotherapy treatments, and other stays were completely unplanned. There were regimens of two drastically different types of chemotherapy treatments designed to improve my health and increase my chances of survival. Although I cannot exactly recall the precise treatment regimens, I absolutely did not enjoy the variations of treatments A & B, my health did indeed improve.

After that difficult and arduous several months, my oncologist again performed tests, only this time to gauge how well the complete treatment worked. She entered the room with another nurse. They were both wearing huge smiles. The doctor uttered the words: **"The cancer is gone and you're in TOTAL REMISSION!!"**

I slightly showed a little more emotion than from the initial diagnosis, but I was ecstatic internally. She even remarked about the display of stoicism from me throughout the entire battle. The nurse said, "I knew you would beat it." She shouted the phrase with joy on her face! She was right; the Holy Spirit obliterated the cancer *through* the oncologist as *well as me.* **YES!!!!!**

> **The Lord is close to the brokenhearted; he rescues those whose spirits are crushed.—(Psalms 34:18)**

The Transition

I moved closer to my family in Indianapolis, Indiana in October of 2012 after the cancer ordeal. I realized that I would have to release the hidden resentment directed at my family. I unwittingly developed a 'root of bitterness' towards them throughout the whole cancer ordeal.

I was completely isolated during one of the darkest times of my life. Our common enemy (the devil) took FULL advantage of that situation. Therefore, we must be very aware of his lurking presence because he will pounce at any opportune moment.

> **Get rid of all bitterness, rage and anger, brawling and slander, along with every form of malice. Be kind and compassionate to one another, forgiving each other, just as Christ GOD *forgave you.*— (Ephesians 4:31)**

> **Stay alert! Watch out for your great enemy, the devil. He prowls around LIKE a roaring lion, looking for someone to devour. Stand firm against him, and be strong in your**

faith. Remember that your family of believers all over the world is going through the same kind of suffering you are.—(1 Peter 5: 8-9)

I had a very brief stint in the hospital due to additional health complications, as well as the residual effects of the chemotherapy treatments (like weakness in my limbs).

After evaluation by the hospital staff, it was then determined that I should have further assistance of a long-term nursing home facility to assist me with those health needs. I agreed to the additional care. Because God had 'ordered my steps' from childhood, I instinctively knew He had designed a purpose for my life in choosing a *specific nursing facility.* Despite having no clue as to what all was included in "God's plan," I decided to believe and trust Him.

I'm certain that the apostle Paul didn't find many of his experiences pleasurable, but because he knew he was called by God Himself; he was more pliable in many ways.

God used Pharaoh's hardened heart against His chosen people (The Israelites) when He instructed Moses to tell Pharaoh to let His people go. God would later use Judas Iscariot to betray Jesus for the crucifixion. Likewise, He uses you and me, but God factors in the use of free will.

> **And we know that God causes everything to work together for the good of those who love God and are called according to his purpose for them.—(Romans 8:28)**

God's Plan

My stay in the nursing facility lasted several months, but that stay was cushioned by the presence of my mother. Though several of the hospital staff recommended the nursing facility, the specific place was completely my choice and I chose to be close to my mom.

No, Not THAT One!

During 2013, while in the nursing facility, I experienced a high fever, followed by chills and a few other symptoms. That situation alerted both staff as well as yours truly that some serious medical issue was lurking.

My loving sister made the decision to have me transferred to the hospital for some tests to be performed. Thankfully, she made that call quickly because the culprit was then identified as *a burst and/or ruptured appendix.* Emergency surgery is required for this procedure since the infection from the rupture can get into your bloodstream, causing sepsis and possible death.

Speaking of death, that is *exactly* what happened to me on the operating table. The coding (which is the medical terminology) happened *three separate times!* However, it was **Congestive Heart Failure (CHF)** that would have appeared on my death certificate.

Once more, **GOD** intervened. Somehow (I will not hazard a guess because frankly, *I do not know),*

I successfully escaped ANOTHER of the enemy's attempts on my life.

In March of 2014, I relocated out of the nursing facility where I endured several different roommates and personalities. I moved to an assisted living facility in East Indianapolis, where I currently reside.

Fast forward to the spring of 2017. I wanted to begin filling the God-sized hole in my soul that only *He* could fill. I discovered the strong presence of the Holy Spirit while watching *Trinity Broadcasting Network.* I was immediately hooked to a specific church and soon thereafter I purchased two series from that ministry, led by a very youthful, yet relatable passionate pastor.

Over the course of approximately two and a half years, I have started shedding my selfish behavior and lending my time to volunteer work for that same church. I am also active in a couple of sermon discussion groups. The groups gather online through a platform called **Zoom Cloud Meetings**. Those meetings are conducted virtually, but individuals also have the option to meet in person locally as well.

Life is still challenging post-cancer ordeal; however it is also ***MUCH* BETTER.** God began His perfect plan of placing an online community of like-minded believers on my spiritual path. I became best friends for life with a fellow follower of Christ in 2019. Several other significant and authentic relationships were also formed and cultivated through the online platform. It was Isaiah 43:18-19 in FULL EFFECT...

> **Forget the former things; do not dwell on the past. SEE, I am doing a new thing! Now it springs up; do you not perceive it? I am making a way in the wilderness and streams in the wasteland.—(Isaiah 43:18-19)**

CHAPTER II

NEW SONG (MELANIE)

He put a new song in my mouth, a hymn of praise to our God. Many will see and fear the Lord and put their trust in him.—(Psalms 40:3)

MY STORY IS NOT ONE I AM INNATELY proud of, but this is not about my pride. This is about transformation and restoration.

A mom and her young son decided to move to an unknown place in the middle of nowhere because God suggested it. After years of struggle with alcohol abuse, codependency, and loss of direction I was finally stepping into freedom from those strongholds. God showed me there is a way. He ALWAYS makes a way.

> **The Lord had said to Abram, "Go from your country, your people and your father's household to the land I will show you."—(Genesis 12:1)**

"My Modern Day Ur"

I heard God's truth, and I began clinging to every promise in each song, message, and scripture. I decided to move forward and trust God with every step. "You are a light unto my path and a lamp unto my feet" (Psalms 119:105).

Everyone thought I was already a little zany, but those who knew me thought I had finally gone off the edge, even if I was truly sober. However, I knew the cravings for alcohol had been lifted and God was directing my steps. I made a commitment to rely on His direction rather than coping with a substance.

Not long after recovery, things began to happen for me with my finances that were truly miraculous. There is no other explanation! The agencies that had put me through so much struggle had finally come through, and I was awarded back pay. I then could become intentional about finding a home for me and my son. I had put Lukas in a group home for over a year, due to my inability to manage my own life; much less his. I yearned to find a place my son and I could call home so that neither of us ever had to be separated again.

The stress of living in the Bay Area of California really took a toll me. Even with a stable career as an interpreter for the deaf, I could not stay on top of my finances. I did not want to continue down the same path. I knew I needed a major change, and God would show me where I needed to go.

> **In their hearts humans plan their course, but the Lord establishes their steps. (Proverbs 16:9)**

When You Decide

I began looking for an affordable home and a place where we would be happy and content. My three adult children had begun lives of their own. Both of my daughters were engaged to be married, and my son Joshua was living in Reno, Nevada with friends. After doing an online search of homes in my price range, I decided to head up to Portola, CA on Memorial Day Weekend 2017. I will never forget that very "memorable" holiday.

I spoke with the real estate agent and made an offer on the home I believed was exactly what we needed. The process of purchasing this home began, and after lots of twists and turns the escrow finally closed on July 19th, 2017—Lukas's thirteenth birthday. I was officially a homeowner. The details of this event were simply amazing. God was present and strategic with every phone call and stroke of the pen. He promised He would make a way, and He did.

Ironically, after I told my son Joshua we would be moving closer to him, he informed me he had to move from the place he was living. Therefore; it would not just be me and Lukas, Joshua would be moving in as well. I could not be more thrilled. It was another one of God's gracious blessings.

You see, Joshua had a difficult time when I chose to put Lukas in a home and move out of our home in Discovery Bay, CA. I was worried we would never be close again. However, God once again allowed a victory in that relationship and we three were reunited. I am so thankful for the time we had to restore our relationship. Lukas adores his older brother Joshua and he will always be my youngest son's hero. This was God's favor at work for my youngest child. I am sure Lukas and God had many conversations about him being reunited with his big brother and sisters. He lost all of them for long enough, and God was preparing a way for even more blessings.

While living in Northern California a few months and celebrating the upcoming weddings with my daughters, I began to get overwhelmed again. The home was not what I had expected with several issues that I was not aware of once we settled in. I began to doubt myself as well as the decisions I made. But God stepped in and pulled me from the quicksand (if you will) once again and placed me firmly. He never fails me and He always remains faithful.

> **He lifted me out of the slimy pit, out of the mud and mire; he set my feet on a rock and gave me a firm place to stand. (Psalms 40:2)**

I eventually got through the difficulties of becoming a homeowner. I joined my sisters from our church "Renewed Life" in the Bay Area on a retreat. On that retreat my friend Janet told me about an online church she had been watching and thought I would enjoy as well. She knew we had moved to a remote rural area and there may be difficulties in finding a church. She introduced me to a specific church based out of North Carolina.

As soon as I got home, I began to watch this deeply passionate and intense pastor online. He has a dynamic way of speaking and sharing God's truth.

I immediately began to search for ways I could get involved and become part of this online community. I was part of some Facebook groups that had been incredibly helpful while I was adjusting to being a special needs mom. I figured that this online church would be similar and at the minimum, get me through until I could find a local church. But it was *so* much more than I expected.

First, I reached out to a young woman named Melissa as I inquired about volunteering opportunities within the church and she asked me to email her my story. That connection with Melissa has continued to flourish as time and volunteer opportunities have moved forward.

I joined a team for welcoming new believers at this church. My specific role is to reach out to those individuals who had watched the online experience and decided to follow Jesus. They had been in contact with another volunteer, but after a couple of weeks we reached out again to make sure they were on track with their decision and encouraged them to get more involved. The experience was pure joy to me! I loved our team and I am so thankful it was my introduction to various other online communities.

Soon after volunteering on this team for the church, I joined a group where we would discuss the sermon from the prior week. This is a group of people that meet once a week to discuss the sermon or any other curriculum our church offered. The groups are inclusive, yet specific to any preference. For example: men, women, married, single, people who currently reside in another country, etc.

We also have groups that discuss a surplus of books by Christian authors, including our own pastor. I loved this community of beautiful people and could not wait to meet with them every week. Admittedly, it was awkward at first as I was unfamiliar with using Zoom for meetings, but I quickly learned how to navigate and stay focused as we met each week.

Since this transition and miraculous provision by my Father in heaven, He has done so much more. The following winter, circumstances brought my daughter and her husband here to live with me as well until they could save money and move into their own home. Just a few months later, my other daughter and her husband moved here as well. The reunion story continued as we were all able to share weekly sushi nights and enjoy the outdoor activities Reno/Tahoe had to offer. God has done a miracle of restoration in my life that I never expected. He has allowed Lukas to progress in ways I never imagined possible.

Lukas was isolated in classrooms with his other school districts, but here he is fully included with all the other students in school. He is both well-known and well liked, and the lives of many have changed just by simply meeting him. There are countless ways this leap of faith was miraculous. It would take another book to list them all, but the biggest miracle of all was staying connected to my online community, which is why I believe the rest of the miracles followed.

I never expected to meet the extended family I have through this experience. I still cannot believe I have friends all over the world who send audio prayers and write music for my son—prayers for healing and songs speaking joy and peace. I am incredibly thankful that God not only made a way through the valley, but He parted the sea as I embarked on this journey. He kept His promise, and He gave me above and beyond what I asked or imagined.

> **For I know the plans I have for you, declares the Lord, plans to prosper you and not to harm you, plans to give you hope and a future. Then you will call on me and come and pray to me, and I will listen to you. You will seek me and find me when you seek me with all your heart.—(Jeremiah 29:11-13)**

CHAPTER III

Loved (Rob)

There is no fear in *love.* But perfect *love* drives out fear, because fear has to do with punishment. The one who fears is not made perfect in *love.*—(1 John 4:18)

IT WAS A MONDAY MUCH LIKE ANY other Monday, but that day was a little different. To be perfectly honest, as I write this chapter, I do not even feel I should be here. Why exactly? Because two and a half years ago, I was sitting right where I am now, but I was a beggar. Begging God for mercy.

The Internal Isis

There was a war going on in my head, in my heart, and in my spirit. I was losing battles with negative self-talk ***big time!*** I was living in a constant nightmare being tortured by fear, guilt, and shame. I had already thought about killing myself on numerous occasions. Not that I wanted to die at all; rather, I just wanted the pain to go away.

In fact, I wanted to live, and I desired to be free from all the horrendous things I had done in my life. I wanted to be free to live in love with my family. I knew nothing of Jesus Christ, and I really did not know anything about God. I would judge those who did so by thinking to myself, "What's so wrong with them that they have to run to God?"

But I had nowhere else to turn, except towards God. I had simply gone too far in the opposite direction, and a one-hundred-eighty-degree turn was needed. So, I decided to fall on my knees and beg for mercy from a God I was not even sure could hear me. Then, much like Saul's (apostle Paul) encounter with God on the Damascus road

(Acts 9:3-8), it hit me. My ears became deaf with a ringing, and I could not hear clearly apart from the constant ringing in my ears. I do not know what made me ask, but I asked God, "Is this you?" Soon after, my question was answered by God and a rush of peace fell over me.

El Roi (God who sees)

For the first time in months, there was no panic. There was a silent, yet all-encompassing **hope** and I believed I was heard. I knew I had to go deeper and find the source of this peace. So, I got myself ready for work, hopped in my truck, and beelined it to the nearest religious shop.

> **"Ask and it be given to you; seek and you will find; knock and the door will be opened to you." For everyone who asks receives; the one who seeks finds; and to the one who knocks, the door will be opened. (Matthew 7:7-8)**

I needed something; anything, so I grabbed myself a few prayer books off the shelves and a catholic bracelet. I have since replaced the catholic bracelet with another one, but it is still there, and I still own one.

I continued my route back to work in my truck with a significant difference. This time I was armed with my service weapon, prayer books, and a *bracelet.* As I was driving, I thought to myself, "Let me see what the internet has to offer in terms of powerful sermons on anxiety, depression and stress."

Well, the internet dispensed a result that was in hindsight, the turning point of my life. This sermon resonates with anyone wrestling with shame from doubt and unbelief. From the very beginning of the sermon, Jesus has completed the crucifixion and has been resurrected from the grave, yet He sets out on what we would describe as a leisurely stroll. However, there's "always" purpose in everything that Jesus does.

He meets a discouraged couple along a road called "Emmaus." They were crushed that He was not resurrected when they thought that He would be. But perhaps the Son of Man will be compassionate enough to meet a discouraged couple on their disappointing trip home to a small village.

After the invitation to dine with the couple for supper, Jesus finally disclosed his identity and their countenance suddenly changed upon the discovery.

Jesus will meet you where you are.

For me, what used to hold us does not hold us anymore.

When he was at the table with them, he took the bread being served, gave thanks, broke it and began to give it to them. Then their eyes were opened, and they recognized him, and he disappeared from their sight.

During this time period, I was forty years old. I have a wife and three children. Two sons, ages twenty-one and twelve, and a daughter, age five. I am in law enforcement as a profession, but ironically, I allowed my own life to slip away. However, unbeknownst to me, **the Holy Spirit** never let me lose my life.

There I was, beaten almost to death in my teens, and oddly enough it was a priest who saved me.

I had quite a few near-death experiences. I have seen friends (both in uniform and not) succumb. Throughout all that I encountered and witnessed; I was still alive.

WHY?

I have been both a horrible husband and a terrible father. But my wife never left me, and my kids still love me. Over time, things started to come back to me. Hindsight is 20/20, right? Events that should have gone wrong but didn't; decisions I made that should have landed me in a few unpleasant places besides my pleasant and fulfilling law enforcement career. You know how they say you see God's work throughout your life in reverse? Well, that is how I view my life now.

I see all the times that God was continually reaching out to me through others, as well as utilizing wise counsel to do so. He was simultaneously rescuing me from dangers and saving my life. Honestly, this has happened more times than I can count. I could go on and on about my story, but it would all lead to this one point:

God is real, God is very good, and He loves EACH of us.

If He would be gracious and merciful enough to save a wretch like me, God will do it for ***anyone!*** I don't know who is reading this, where you have been, what you have done, or what you are currently facing, but I do know this: Jesus paid for it all up there on that 'old rugged cross'.

Whether you have realized or received His grace and mercy yet or not, it has been placed up there on the cross. The Savior of the world made that great exchange for you and me over two thousand years ago, up on a hill called Calvary. His righteousness for our wretchedness *cannot and will not* be undone.

CHAPTER IV

IMPACTFUL (ERIC)

Study and be eager and do your utmost to present yourself to God approved (tested by trial), a workman who has no cause to be ashamed, correctly analyzing and accurately dividing [rightly handling and skillfully teaching] the Word of Truth.—(2 Timothy 2:15)

THERE I WAS IN A DARK CLOSET, BEING touched in areas an eight-year-old boy was not supposed to be touched. Scared and suffocating, not knowing what was going on, I suffered. This grotesque act went on for a few years, in this space as well as others. I lived in the dark, both internally and externally; this created roots deep within which I never imagined would EVER go away. "But God."

From Wounds...

Years before during and after the molestation, I was raised up in a few devil-stomping, Holy Ghost rolling, tongues-speaking Pentecostal churches surrounded by amazing parents, family, and friends. But despite all things religious, I continued to live this deep, dark-rooted secret which was causing me to rot from the inside out.

A few years later, an image of an 'adult magazine' was seemingly tattooed in my memory. The more I dug deeper into these images of women, the more I started to sink into sin. Lust began to leak into all my relationships. I was unfaithful to every girlfriend I had, and I began using girls for only one thing. Without being too detailed, you can utilize your imagination to determine for yourself what that one thing was.

Fast forward to March 4, 2000, in a little church in Illinois, where the pastor asked for anyone to raise their hand and repeat after him. I sensed a nudge, so I shot my hand up and the pastor said, "I see that hand." It felt like it was simultaneously the best and worst decision I felt I ever made, because the next nineteen years were nothing short of spectacular, sorrowful, and full of hills and valleys.

Here I go, getting married in 2002 with all this extra baggage inside still piling up, as I am dealing with symptoms of darkness without ever exploring the *root causes.* Despite being '*saved, healed and delivered*' through my confession to Christ and subsequent baptism, those dark moments were never exposed to light.

Hurt People Hurt Others

2004 came and as I was newly divorced, I began having affairs with married women. My viewing of pornography increased (this was going on for years). I was never faithful in a relationship, but my appetite for this lifestyle was next level. I did not seem to care that I was hurting inside. I did not know how to numb the God-sized hole disguised as intense pain. I attempted to numb it by filling that void with porn, sex, sports, alcohol, etc.

In late summer, on August 1st 2004, I met the woman I prayed about when I was a child: and I would come to meet her; Renee Christine Hatfield. I knew *instantly* she was the one, as we were set up on a blind date during the summer. Both of our mothers planned and planned the date for six months. It scared me nearly to death inside knowing she was *"the one"!* For roughly six months, things between us were going quite well. The relationship was nearly perfect until I returned to my self-destructive habits. I decided to move on from Renee in early January 2006.

I decided that being *intentional* was a much better option for me, so I dated another woman with the right motives. We made plans for marriage, and I was going to wait for her to finish college (she was younger). I was even traditional in asking her father's permission beforehand, but he said "NO," so I moved on. Then I started dating another lady before breaking it off on Christmas Eve. That very same night I met up with Renee, and the rest (as the phrase goes) is history.

More Than Coffee Percolating

Renee and I reunited in December of 2006, and I did not want to look back, but the biggest storms were brewing, and I would be FORCED to uncover the past. In November 2007, we had our eldest daughter, Erica Christine, weighing seven pounds, twelve ounces. Our second daughter, Reese Eve, was born in March 2010, weighing in at seven pounds, six ounces.

Accompanying the two wonderful additions, the chaos continued. There were plenty of lies, and drinking habits formed throughout those years. My destructive choices occurred all while we were going to church, praying, and reading the Bible.

In the fall of 2012, I had yet another affair, except this time I was the married one. I was an alcoholic by the very definition of the word. Definitely suffered depression and my life was slowly spiraling downward—but my life was about to be forever impacted in a positive way.

> **And I am convinced and sure of this very thing, that He Who began a good work in you will continue until the day of Jesus Christ [right up to the time of His return], developing [that good work] and perfecting and bringing it to full completion in you.—(Philippians 1:6)**

To Being Reinstated...

In 2016 I was holding the affair, the molestation, all these lies, and so much more inside of me until I finally came clean. That was a very *tough* decision to make, but it was also ***quite freeing!*** Shortly afterwards, the shift began as I saw a thirty-second clip on Facebook of a ***deeply passionate*** and ***energetic pastor***. We were still going through alcoholism, the affair, a failed suicide attempt, and a whole lot more, but we started to DVR his sermons on Trinity Broadcasting Network. We also decided to purchase resource materials.

As we went through the difficulties of our combined pasts, we got worse externally but internally God was massaging our hearts. As He began to work on my wife and me individually, our marriage was restored like God originally intended.

In February 2017, we ***uprooted*** from Illinois to North Carolina (that is a book by itself). Currently we are in transition from North Carolina to Iowa (book #2), but through it all I've learned God is faithful even when we are faithless.

> **The saying is sure and worthy of confidence: If we have died with Him, we shall also live with Him. If we endure, we shall also reign with Him. If we deny and disown and reject Him, He will also deny, disown and reject us. If we are faithless [do not believe and are untrue to Him], He remains true (faithful**

to His word and His righteous character), for He cannot deny Himself.—(2 Timothy 2:11-13)

If it had not been for God's grace and that thirty-second clip on Facebook, I certainly would not have been courageous enough to tell a portion of my story. If it weren't for God leading me to become a part of this ***'Untold Love Story'*** unfolding, things in my life would be a **whole lot different!**

I am also participating in one of the sermon discussion groups like you read in Melanie's story. I am equipped with all the connections, community, and care from people all over the world. It is an opportunity I do not take for granted. I am not where I need to be but thank God I am not where I used to be. Thank You, heavenly Father, for surrounding me with this awesome display of love!

CHAPTER V

New Creation (Suzie)

> **Therefore, if any person is [ingrafted] in Christ (the Messiah) he is a new creation (a new creature altogether); the old [previous moral and spiritual condition] has passed away. Behold, the fresh and new has come!—(2 Corinthians 5:17)**

As I reflect on 2019 while simultaneously ushering in another decade, I realize I have the ***Best Family Ever!*** Not in the conventional sense, however, most of this family I have yet to meet. They primarily reside in the United States.

I also have family globally. This is the reality and power of an online extended family.

Small Beginnings

Growing up in Northern Ireland was a challenging childhood experience. I endured a plethora of medical issues as the product of a premature birth. Family life was not great, and neither was school life. I suffered at various schools due to constant bullying, both at the hands of classmates and those of a close relative. We did go to church when I was a child, but it was more out of routine than faith and belief in God.

In my early teens, I spent my Sundays going to practically every denomination of church. Looking back, I realize I was searching for God, but I never found Him. Instead of discovering and developing a personal relationship with God, I kept running into religious rules and regulations. Overall, the loudest message from everyone was that I just never quite measured up!

And He said, go out and stand on the mount before the Lord. And behold, the Lord passed by, and a great and strong wind rent the mountains and broke in pieces the rocks before the Lord, but the Lord was not in the wind; and after the wind an earthquake, but the Lord was not in the earthquake; And after the earthquake a fire, but the Lord was not in the fire; and after the fire [a sound of gentle stillness and] a still, small voice. – (1 Kings 19:11-12)

Fast forward to January 2003: I moved to London a few months earlier to begin my pediatric nursing career. My flat mate (roommate) introduced me to her church, and the initial overwhelming impression was that Christians could be happy. Moreover, a church can be a *joyful* and positive place.

This led to me doing Alpha, a fantastic Bible-based course where I met so many amazing people from all backgrounds. (**Alpha course creates a space for people to bring friends for a conversation about faith, life, and God.**)

The biggest revelation to me was that God loved me ***as is.*** He was not some scary being that I continually had to prove myself to; He loved me.

Due to substandard health, I could no longer practice my nursing career. In addition to that debilitating career blow, I also changed churches because I was unable to travel. Thereafter, I began to attend a smaller contemporary church nearby.

By June 2013, other circumstances led me back to live with my parents in Northern Ireland. Due to my declining health and other personal reasons, attending church was no longer an option.

Initially my parents lived in a small village and our home then was even facing a Baptist church (God has a sense of humor). Later that first summer back home, I signed up to do an online Bible study with Proverbs 31 Ministries. In addition to the study, one of the study leaders did a blog on her church. The blog post sparked my curiosity and as such I began my spiritual journey to a church in Charlotte, North Carolina. In case you are wondering, that is over thirty-five hundred miles away (physically) from the village in Northern Ireland (where I now live).

The blog was week one of a new sermon series that will remain nameless. Within a few weeks, I was inextricably hooked. The most amazing thing is that I felt truly connected to this community back then—yet on paper, I had *absolutely* no reason to!

Within the church app were some quite interesting learning materials. There was a streaming service which ran on four hourly cycles, and at the top of the hour, the current sermon. On Saturdays and Sundays, there was the live stream of the worship experience. I watched every experience on my tiny iPod touch! Talk about H-U-N-G-R-Y for the living Word of God!

But how are people to call upon Him Whom they have not believed [in Whom they have no faith, on

Whom they have no reliance]? And how are they to believe in Him [adhere to, trust in, and rely upon Him] of Whom they have never heard? And how are they to hear without a preacher? – (Romans 10:14-15)

The pastor of this megachurch made the bible come alive for me, much more than anyone has ever before—especially the Old Testament. I began writing all over my bible and I most likely have listened to and watched every *single* sermon on the older version of the church's app. Aside from the sermons and the music, the structure of the church (from volunteering, participating, and giving), all gave me a deeper understanding of how the church should be. Still, I knew that no church is *perfect.*

Beauty for Ashes

At the beginning of my search to uncover my spiritual journey, I yearned to serve or be in small group discussions. After three years of faithfulness watching online, my prayers to connect were answered; the *official start* of **a virtual campus!**

And it had been quite a ride. I could not wait to serve and join a group that discussed various sermons and more, all from my tiny iPod. I am profoundly grateful that I get the opportunity to serve ***in this capacity.***

Serving online has given me opportunities to expand my family ***worldwide!*** Despite reservations with the opposite sex, God placed four amazing men in my life that allowed me to be me, without asking or expecting to know my full story.

This past couple of years has not been easy for me. My dad died suddenly in May 2019. My mum, dad, and I woke up on this day like any other "regular" day. Yet, within a few hours my world was changed forever.

After trying to save my dad's life until the ambulance crews came, there were two people I wanted to speak to in the world right there in that moment. The first was my cousin, who lives in Malaysia and is seven hours ahead of me. The second person was Christina, who lives in Ohio. She is my BFF (best friend forever) and FFF (faith friend forever). We have yet to meet and she is five hours behind my time.

I wanted to speak to her so much, but in my haziness, I forgot that she would be asleep. When I did get to speak to her within an hour of my dad passing away, poor Christina was barely awake as I told her the devastating news. She cried with me, screamed and burst into tears with me. She then stepped in and got all my group members together to pray and made the church staff aware of the situation as well.

Another member of the church community went through a tragedy at the same time. One of the online directors arranged a prayer meeting for the leaders to pray over me and this other family. This is the true reality of what an online campus can be. Personally, I will always be grateful for all my extended family in getting me through this year. I know that if the online campus ended tomorrow, many of the relationships I have made would still stand forever.

Speaking of friendships lasting forever, one day soon Christina and I will meet, and there had better be a box of tissues on hand.

> **Trust in the Lord with all your heart and lean not on your own understanding; in all your ways submit to him, and he will make your paths straight.—(Proverbs 3:5-6)**

A Prayer for the Ephesians

> **For this reason, I kneel before the Father, from whom every family in heaven and on earth derives its name. I pray that out of his glorious riches he may strengthen you with power through his Spirit in your inner being, so that Christ may dwell in your hearts through faith. And I pray that you, being rooted and established in love, may have power, together with all the**

Lord's holy people, to grasp how wide and long and high and deep is the love of Christ, and to know this love that surpasses knowledge—that you may be filled to the measure of all the fullness of God.

Now to him who is able to do immeasurably more than all we ask or imagine, according to his power that is at work within us, to him be glory in the church and in Christ Jesus throughout all generations, for ever and ever! Amen.—(Ephesians 3:14-21)

CHAPTER VI

Expectant (Devra)

Do not burn out; keep yourselves fueled and aflame. Be alert servants of the Master, cheerfully *expectant*. Do not quit in hard times; pray all the harder. Help needy Christians; be inventive in hospitality.—(Romans 12:11-13)

I *WAS* A WRETCHED WOMAN; I FELT LIKE A nobody, a reject, and after many failed attempts to pull myself up, the Lord stepped in and redeemed me.

Satan came for me early as he has done the very same thing in the bible. My childhood was laced with every type of abuse—physical, sexual, and mental. My parents were good at dropping us kids off at church (for which I am forever grateful). I even attended a private Christian school when it opened in our hometown of Cottonwood, AZ. For all the attacks that came against me, God always provided a way for me to the light. I was diagnosed with ovarian cancer at the age of fourteen and told I would never have children... only to become a teenage mother at seventeen, married to an abusive husband at eighteen, divorced, and a single parent of three babies by the age of twenty-three. Let that information sink in for a bit...

I returned to the church—yes, *"the church"*—and started focusing on checking off the boxes that make you a good, respectable person according to religion. I went back to school in my late twenties while simultaneously working my way up the corporate ladder. I donated the appropriate amount to charity. You know, surface clean!

A House (of Worship) Divided

The church fell apart and the people in it scattered; like I said, I returned to the church, not to my ***Savior.*** So, when the church began its collapse, my church attendance was something that just fell away to the side. I was working, making money, and raising kids. Then the subprime mortgage crash came, and my career with it. My mother had moved to another state; my sister had followed her, and they convinced me to move to Texas as well. I packed up the two youngest, while the oldest remained in college at home, and moved to what might as well have been a foreign country to me: the south! The culture shock was more than my middle son could handle and he left to live with his father. It would be just me and the youngest on this journey.

> **Now, Jesus supernaturally perceived their thoughts and motives, so he confronted them by telling them a parable:**

"Any kingdom that fights against itself will end up in ruins. And *any* family of community splintered by strife will fall apart."—(Matthew 12:25)

"An Angel of Darkness Posing as Light"

After a couple of years, I had built a home and began to carve out a life for myself in Orange, TX. An opportunity came for me to better my financial state and I pounced on it. However, that opportunity came at a high cost, and I found myself chained to a deal with pure evil. I was now in my mid-forties and had unwittingly entered a battle that would cost me my career, reputation, my finances, my health, and my family. My superior used his authority, manipulation, and occasionally physical restraint to try to force me into a relationship with him. All the harassment occurred while I was combating a "state declared disaster," which was the terminal I was managing.

But God...

The state came in and set up a command unit onsite. After all, this was a *profoundly serious* crisis in and of itself. I was working twelve to sixteen hours every day; I could not even go to the bathroom without my boss being at the door waiting for me to get out.

During that difficult time, hurricane Harvey (August 2017) also wreaked havoc and it was looking like my home would flood so I was allowed to leave with a crew and sandbag my home. I was to return then, but God had another plan; the roads flooded before I could return to work and I was trapped away from work and away from my home, which did flood. That storm provided me a break from the constant berating from my superior, and when the flood waters receded it also provided me a physical release from all the anger, frustration, and rage I was feeling towards my superior.

He was a master manipulator, so even my family took his side! My own son left me to move in with him and his crew at a hotel. The state eventually removed themselves from the terminal and that is when the situation took a turn for the worse at work; he took my money, my title, and forced me to stay in a private office to get my money back. We argued relentlessly over safety concerns, as we were still mitigating a silo that was under nitrogen to suppress reigniting. We lost a soul, performing work I was adamantly against. I was informed after the loss that, according to the company, I had been reinstated to manager just before the death, thus making me responsible for it legally. I broke down, completely broke down, and had no one—only God to turn to for compassion.

I had pushed myself to continue with work. I motivated myself for my son, and for the employees under my charge, but my body began rebelling against itself. I did not understand the *strange and bizarre* new symptoms—symptoms such as trembling uncontrollably, inability to speak, loss of vision, total impairment of cognitive abilities. I eventually ended up unable to leave my home, suffering from what I have now come to know as Complex PTSD (Post Traumatic Stress

Disorder). It is a medical term that basically means old wounds that never healed had merged with the fresh wounds being inflected on me, and my body was locked in fight or flight mode.

My oldest son had started suffering with anxiety and depression in college, so the biggest blessing of this was that we were able to bond on *much* deeper level. This uninvited set of circumstances was the catalyst for empathy between us. By being vulnerable, he trusted me enough to speak to me about his wounds. We had a wonderful year of video calls and daily chats, and even a few trips together. Lasting fond memories ensued.

It is a year that I cherish and one I am forever grateful for. We talked about my progress and how Jesus was the only way; we talked about dealing with labels once you've been diagnosed with a mental condition; we talked about handling the symptoms, and he knew I was against modern medicine and chose a more natural approach. We just talked, and I am so oh grateful for that.

As for you, you thought evil against me, but God meant it for good, to bring about many people should be kept alive, as they are this day.—(Genesis 50:20)

In the spring of 2018, I listened to a sermon which inevitably led me to heavily participate in a specific church. That very sermon was an argument I had with my youth pastor back when I was a teen! I was so pumped!

The sermon lit a fire within me. Before long, when offered online volunteering, I had to check it out and started serving. Everyone kept talking about the variety of small groups that also met online, so I checked into it and said, ***"Sign me up!"*** What a blessing! I had no idea how much of a blessing it would turn out to be for me.

God's Plan

The Lord has since shown me that all my trials have paved paths that have enabled me to travel down a detoured road that would connect me with others in a way I could not before. I thank God I was connected to the body of Christ through all of it, and I do not believe I would have been able to get so connected had it not all been online! It was surreal how much support I received from the body of Christ!

> **So now I live with the confidence that there is nothing in the universe with the power to separate us from God's love. I am convinced that his love will triumph over death, fallen angels, or dark rulers in the heavens. There is nothing in our present or future circumstances that can weaken his love. There is no power above or beneath us - no power that could ever be found in the universe that can distance us from God's passionate love, which is lavished upon us through our**

Lord Jesus, the Anointed One!—(Romans 8:28-29)

The Shift

I transitioned jobs and completed the work on the house prior to putting it up for sale. Things were looking up for me; however, at the beginning of 2019, I received a call informing me my oldest son was missing and suicidal.

Had I not been involved in and connected to an online community, I shudder to think of where I would be—or if I would even be at all. But I did have connections, and my very first phone call was to my virtual group leader. Within minutes, I was on a video conference call with women all around the world, praying, crying out to the Lord for my son on my behalf. That sense of comfort and support strengthened me and encouraged me in the Lord. ***What love!***

Later that evening at home I felt a rip in my stomach so strong it brought me to my knees. I cried out to God and begged Him for the feeling

I felt not to be true. Then the Lord reminded me of a dream He had given me after my son was born and it comforted me. I knew then that God's perfect will had been done.

My son's car was found that night at the Grand Canyon, and his body was found a couple days later. Found in my son's car was an unopened bottle of whiskey and all the books of the Bible, including the 'dead sea' scrolls and such. **MY GOD!** What a *very symbolic* message he left in his car! I know the Lord led me here for such a time as this. I am forever grateful to the Lord and for those brothers and sisters in Christ that continue to choose to obey Him.

> **The Lord is close to all whose hearts are crushed by pain, and he is always ready to restore the repentant one.—(Psalms 34:18)**

My home in Texas has flooded again, but it flooded with restoration as well. An overflow of things lost, things stolen, things forgotten!

Even now as I write this, healing and restoration are happening in my family, my two younger sons, my mother, sister, and brother-in-law! The Lord is so, so good! I know that nothing can ever separate me from the goodness and faithfulness of our Heavenly Father (Romans 8:38)!

I now lead a couple of groups, including a intercessory team for prayer and a smaller, intimate group for the church, and I have been able to return the precious gift of going before the Father for others. In this short time of service, I have been privileged to go to the Father and witness God's mighty power work in the lives of our brothers and sisters in Christ Jesus.

CHAPTER VII

"It Is Finished" (Amber)

When Jesus had tasted it, he said, "*It is finished!*" Then he bowed his head and gave us his spirit.— (John 19:30)

I AM CRYING PROFUSELY AFTER READING everyone's stories. Tears of sadness turned into tears of joy as each testimony truly is a unique display of our Father's love. His hand is on our lives from day one, and as Rob said, "that's often seen in hindsight."

This group of testimonies cover such a wide spectrum of hurt and pain, mixed with mistakes, yet still display the "reckless love" of our Savior. He chases us down until we are found. I also noticed a common denominator in everyone's story: upon finding the Lord, they immediately became connected and stayed that way.

I have found that to be true in my life as well. We need community and people to walk this journey with us. If Jesus himself had twelve disciples, how much more do we need a group of believers to surround ourselves with?

> **Two are better than one; because they have a good reward for their labor.**
>
> **For if they fall, the one will lift up his fellow: but woe to him that is alone when he falleth; for he hath not another to help him up.—(Ecclesiastes 4:9-12)**

Just like the various other stories told in this book, I too found a church online during a tough season in my life.

Though I was born and raised in church, I was hot and cold, on and off in my walk with the Lord my whole life!

In 2015 I rededicated my life, and in February of 2016 I was diagnosed with breast cancer. Months later, I was divorced and a single mom to a three-year-old daughter. Instead of running like I did in the past when things got tough, I truly found Jesus. The prayers of others carried me and kept me afloat. I began searching online and ran across a sermon by the same young and fiery pastor everyone else in the book has referred to. It was the exact word I needed, and the Lord began changing my heart.

> **A new heart will I give you and a new spirit will I put within you, and I will take away the stony heart out of your flesh and give you a heart of flesh. And I will put my Spirit within you and cause you to walk in My statutes, and you shall heed My ordinances and do them.**
> **- Ezekiel 36:26-27**

I realized I was bound by the chains of religion and had never truly had a relationship with God.

I saw God as rules and regulations, standards to live up to; I believed I would always fail to meet those high expectations!

God knew I would need this real intimate relationship to weather this season of my life, so it felt as if my relationship with Him was in fast forward. I grew so close to Him so quickly. What should have been the darkest time in my life became the most fruitful season. He truly made beauty of the ashes and showed me a Father's love, yet also an intimate love as His bride. He taught me how to surrender past hurts and fears, and He replaced them with intimate trust and love!

He used the church online to plug me in and strategically place people in my life through serving online and online groups. Then the Lord ultimately led me to a church an hour away, which was a "satellite" campus of the church I was involved with online. I began to serve on the welcome team and got connected to people there as well.

I now have the best of both worlds—an online and physical location! As I began to grow in Him, I had other believers to lean on and grow with. I too found that my closest friends were located in states and even countries far away. Only the Lord could weave together our lives in such a beautiful way to make a masterpiece like He does! I still stand in awe of the relationships He has built and continues to build as I continue this journey with Him.

I pray that these stories touch your life as much as they have mine. It rekindles a fire in my heart for those that are lost and/or hurting. The Lord wants this for each of you that have picked up this book. It is no accident; it's a divine part of His plan for your life! Today can be the first day of the rest of your life! I truly pray over each person that reads this book.

If you are not connected to a body of believers, I encourage you to do so. We need each other on this walk; we are not meant to do it alone. I want to also encourage you all to share your story, as those here and I have done. We are overcomers when we share, and our testimony may be the key that unlocks someone else's freedom.

God bless you all!

> **And they have overcame (conquered) him by means of the blood of the Lamb and by the utterance of their testimony, for they did not love and cling to life even when faced with death [holding their lives cheap till they had to die for their witnessing].—(Revelation 12:11)**

CPSIA information can be obtained
at www.ICGtesting.com
Printed in the USA
LVHW091130080221
678693LV00004B/349